every penny counts

Roland Trenary

Grounded Outlet
Kingston   2016

ISBN-13: 9780989577526
ISBN-10: 098957752X
Library of Congress Control Number: 2016931132

Visit us at:
www.groundedoutlet.com
Email us at:
penny@groundedoutlet.com
Watch at:
youtube.com/watch?v=rGDd4CUgGPM

Listen for FREE at:

every
penny
counts

Grandpa says...

My friend, "Dollar" Bill,

was famous.

He always gave a buck

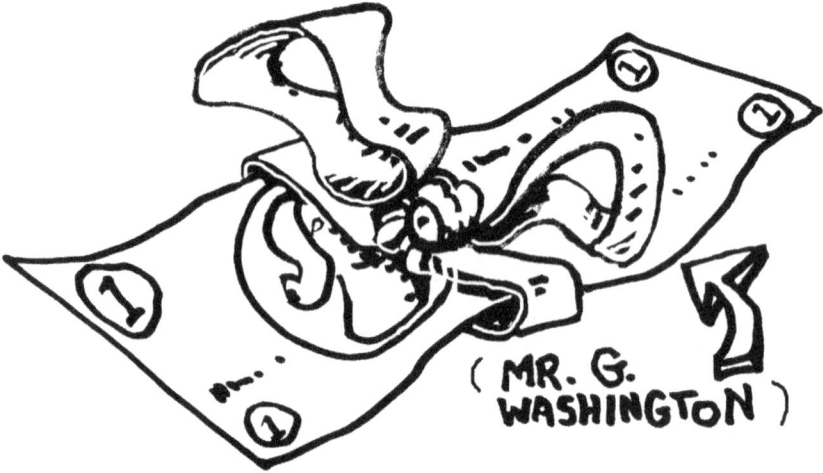

(MR. G.
WASHINGTON)

to any hobo

begging 'round his door.

But since today

I haven't any more.

SPARSE

Now every
penny counts,

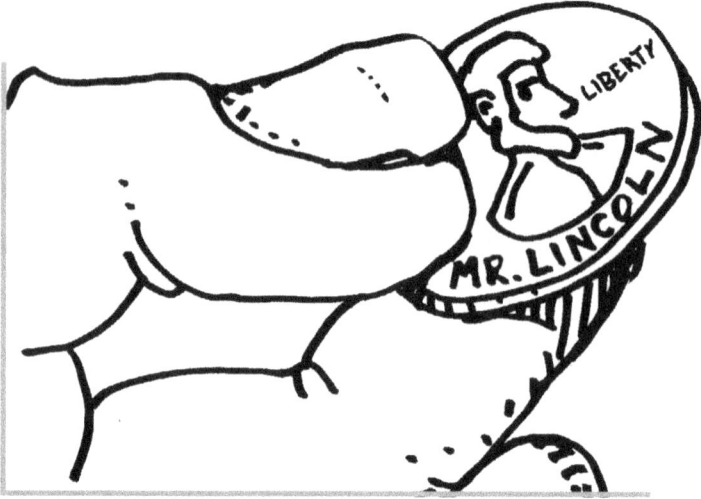

every penny
counts.

Don't deny

the value of a cent!

I recall a time
no one would

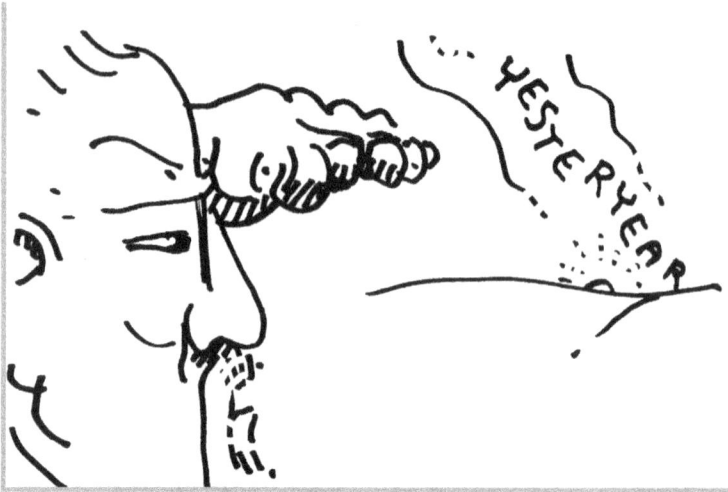

stoop to scoop a dime.

(F. D. ROOSEVELT)   LIBERTY

Now every penny counts,

WINK!

my friend.

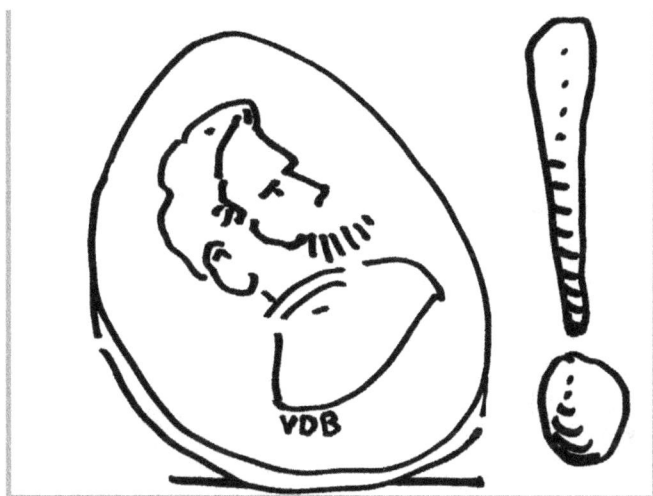

If I had a single nickel

for every time I heard

NOTHING

how
nothin'
ain't worth
nothin'

nowadays,

I'd nod my little head

at the five-cent words they said,

then take each nickel

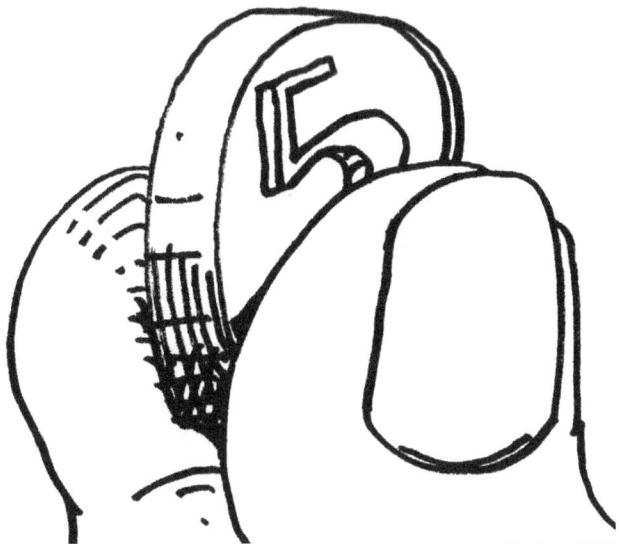

and sock it away.

'Cause every
    penny counts,

every penny
    counts.

Don't deny

the value of a cent.

I recall a time
no one would

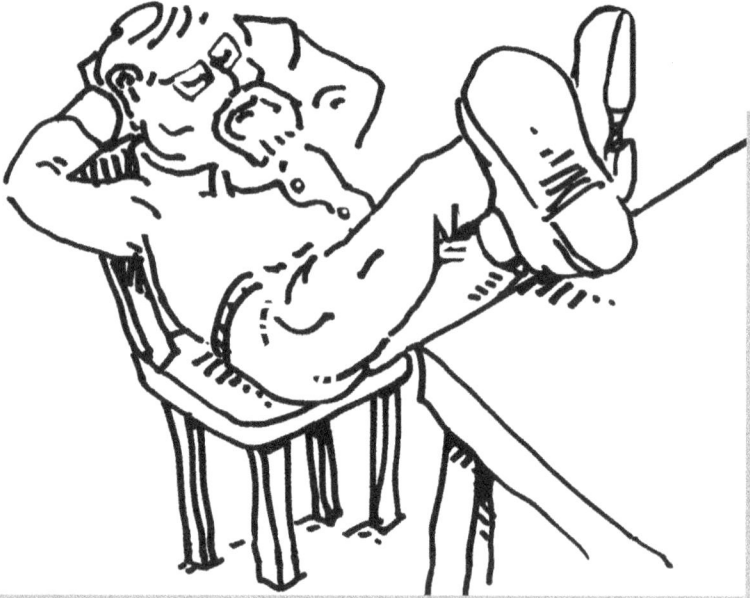

stoop
to scoop a dime.

Now every
penny counts,

my friend.

When
you
think
about
it,

love's
worth
more
than

money.

So are friendship,

FRIENDSH

kinship,

FRIENDS
KINSHIP

happiness,

FRIENDS
KINSHIP
HAPPINE

and health.

FRIEND
KINSHIP
HAPPIN
HEALT

$

Without humor,

nothing's very

f u n n y

But who'd turn down a chance

to wallow in some wealth?

One day
my reluctant
banker

said
I could
see the
vault.

And, don't you know,

I came away
perplexed.

That vault was just as bare as a

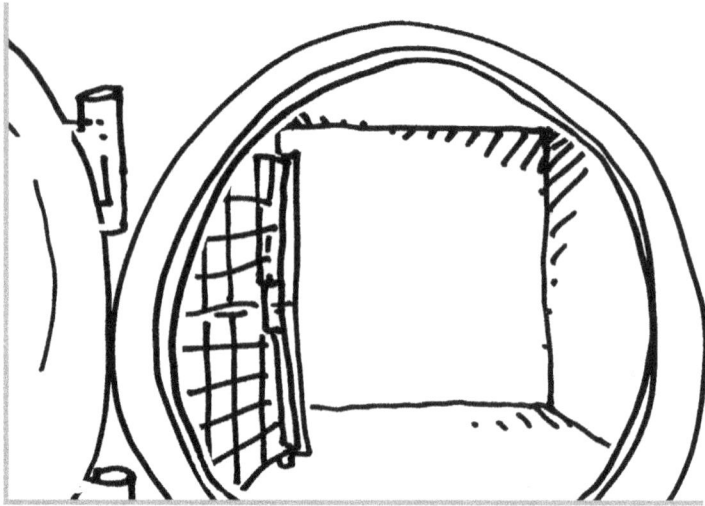

head without a hair!

PLINK!

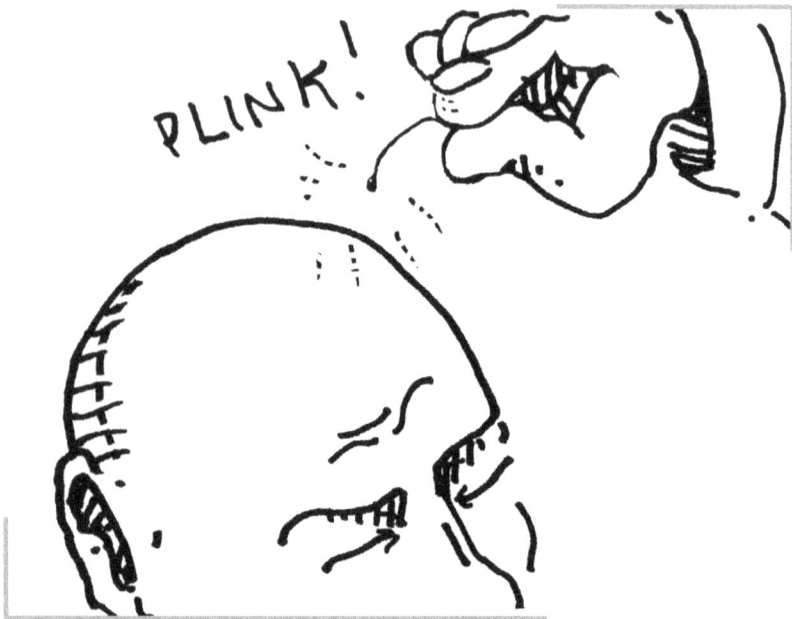

My little piggy's bound to be broke

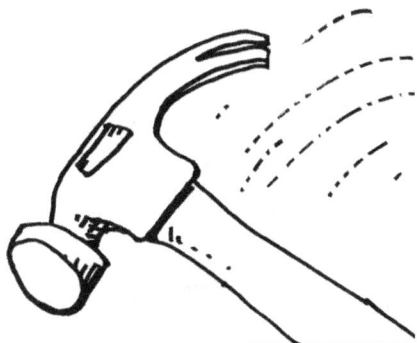

next.

'Cause every
 penny counts,

every penny
 counts.

Don't deny

the value of a cent!

I recall a time no one would

stoop to scoop a dime.

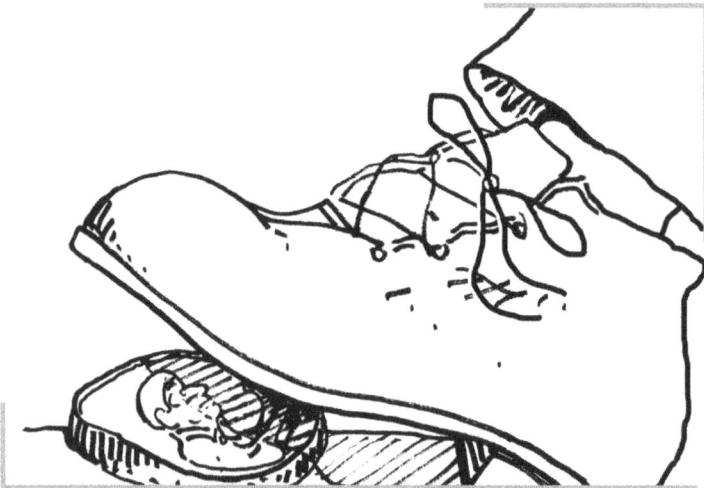

Now every
penny counts,

my
friend.

Every penny counts, every penny counts,

every

penny

counts,

my friend!

The End

(unless you read music...)

EVERY PENNY COUNTS

Roland Trenary

EVERY PENNY COUNTS

31 EV-RY PEN-NY COUNTS, MY FRIEND. WHEN YOU THINK A-BOUT IT LOVE'S WORTH MORE THAN MON-EY. SO ARE

35 FRIEND-SHIP, KIN-SHIP, HAP-PI-NESS AND HEALTH. WITH-OUT HU-MOR NOT-THING'S VER-Y FUN-NY._____ BUT

39 WHO'D TURN DOWN A CHANCE TO WAL-LOW IN SOME WEALTH? ONE DAY MY RE-LUC-TANT BANK-ER SAID

43 I COULD SEE THE VAULT, AND DON'T YOU KNOW I CAME A-WAY PER-PLEXED. THAT VAULT WAS JUST AS BARE AS A

47 HEAD WITH-OUT A HAIR. MY LIT-TLE PIG-GY'S BOUND TO BE BROKE NEXT. NOW EV-RY PEN-NY COUNTS,

51 EV-RY PEN-NY COUNTS. DON'T DE-NY THE VAL-UE OF A CENT. I RE-CALL A TIME NO ONE WOULD

55 STOOP TO SCOOP A DIME. NOW EV-RY PEN-NY COUNTS, MY FRIEND. EV-RY PEN-NY COUNTS,

59 EV - RY PEN-NY COUNTS, EV - RY PEN - NY COUNTS! MY FRIEND.

Also by Roland Trenary:

Fever That Yearns
✳✳✳
Fourteen artfully
original songs.

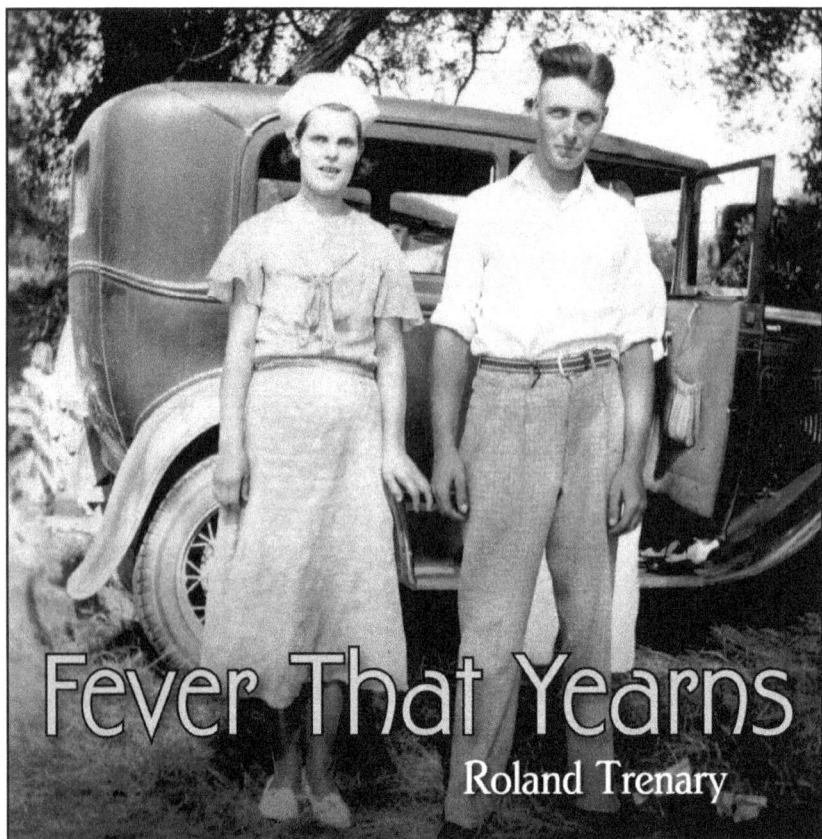

And don't forget:

Mahlon Blaine's SINDBAD
✳✳✳
An intricately rhyming coloring book.

MAHLON BLAINE's SINDBAD

ROLAND TRENARY

www.ingramcontent.com/pod-product-compliance
Lightning Source LLC
Chambersburg PA
CBHW030310030426
42337CB00012B/657